MAKE OPPORTUNITIES COME TO YOU

Learn how to Prepare for, recognize, attract opportunities and Put yourself on the frontline for all round breakthrough

KINGSLEY OBIEFULE

PRAISE FOR THE BOOK

"With this book, it is possible for you…"

Kingsley Obiefule, in a typical and practical way, has woven together a master piece for everyone, especially young people who are still bubbling with energy. His book, "Make Opportunities Come to You," opens its reader, as it did me, to salient practicable truths to becoming a person that makes your dream life possible.

Everyone desires a chance and an opportunity, but anyone who understands the rudiments and intricacies of attracting opportunities especially as it is outlaid in this book is a better person than the others who merely desire. Stop getting-ready for opportunities, and start living ready for opportunities. One opportunity creates a chain of other opportunities by a force of magnetization.

If you want opportunities, you can engage it. Get Kingsley's book to intentionally become a person that typically lives an "opportunities-attracting life." With this book, it is possible for you.

EZRA DANJUMA AKAMA,

Author, Speaker & Curator, The Emergent Hub.

"If you read it and don't get propelled, then, all hope for your personal growth will be lost…"

I read voraciously and I can say that **Make Opportunities Come to You** was well written.

Most times writers neglect to address the role religion and spirituality play in personal development and how we are all affected by them. This book dealt with certain notions that keeps people at a certain point in life, where they do not put in the work required in other to up their growth and visibility game.

This is one book that jerks you and puts fire in your veins. If you read it and don't get propelled, then, all hope for your personal growth will be lost.

DIVINE EZE

Founder Storytellers Boot camp & Author, Authenticity

"Process and implementation philosophy…"

At long last, an audacious expression of the **process and implementation philosophy**, as it brings to light not just the importance of a goal or an idea, but the emphatic importance of the workings thereof, a must read for every 21st century creative mind.

EDDY BRISIBE

BOT Chairman RDI, Convener of Projectdelta Program

"Create and Retain opportunities…"

When you go extra mile, you put yourself way ahead of many when it comes to opportunities. It's the best way to create opportunity. This book will show you exactly how to create and retain opportunities. Great work.

OLADIMEJI OLUTIMEHIN

Author, Millionaire Maker

"Proverbs written in Contemporary Language…"

Explosive and overdosed with uncanny wisdom. This is proverbs written in Contemporary Language.

AMAKA DONALD-IBE

Speaker, Author; Growing your Money Pot, Penny to Plenty.

"To improve your chances of success…"

Make Opportunities Come to You meticulously articulated how you can position, recognize, attract and maximize opportunities that have once eluded you.

To improve your chances of success, this book needs to be in your shelf.

JUSTIN TOCHUKWU

The Brand Surgeon

DEDICATION

I dedicate this piece to every young dreamer in Africa, who wakes up every morning with their dreams right before them, wishing and hoping that one day it becomes a celebrated reality.

I am putting this work out there for you who is going through a certain season you don't understand. You are frustrated with the system, you feel nothing good can come out of you. Maybe you feel you have been betrayed by all you were taught by formal education. I am saying, your dreams and hopes are valid and will come to pass.

To the creative, who is seeking to be known and rewarded for his creativity and solutions. To the creative who has found a solution but yet haven't gotten a way to let the world see him or her, I am saying "wake up, and shine your light."

I am dedicating this work to every young Nigerian and African; the Nigeria and Africa of our dream will emerge. I have seen it, and you are a key player in that revolution.

I am dedicating this to everyone who wants more out of life than what they are currently experiencing.

Table of Contents

INTRODUCTION

Dear friend,

Thank you for picking up this book. Whether it was given to you by someone, or you picked it up somewhere and decided to pass time with it, I want to say thank you.

I know time is precious so I will cut straight to the chase.

I have read quite a number of books and blogs about opportunities. They all make sense in their own way. Many emphasize on the importance of "if you can think it, you can achieve it." I would not want to pretend with you. Many of us have "thought" it and yet, it seems like nothing will ever happen. This leaves us in serious frustration. This is why many people tell you that motivational speakers are scammers. One thing they don't understand is that it's more than just "thinking it." That's just the first part of the equation.

Thinking money doesn't make you have money.

There is no need for you to get over dozed with motivation and yet you do nothing and get zero result. I don't want to be amongst those who are responsible for your motivational obesity. This is why I decided to put this piece together, to show you what to do with that motivation. It's about "being" and "doing". This simply means you would become a certain kind of person which will lead to doing things in a certain kind of way.

Throughout this book, I have promised myself to be honest with you. If you are looking for that kind of miracle book that after reading, things just happen even without you putting in any work, then this is not for you. The book you are holding in your hands is a call to work.

You will definitely find things that doesn't sound like what your pastor told you, what your father told you and all that. I might tamper with your theology, forgive me for that. This book might challenge the conventional things you have always believed. Yes, you might disagree. That's not a problem. But just read with an open mind. Even though my aim is to challenge you to see things from a different perspective, you can decide not to be challenged. I totally get it.

If you are a young person reading this book, you need to pay attention. Everything shared in this book are things that has over time yielded results in the lives of many Africans like you and i. I have practiced them and seen results too. Most of them were not born with spoon in their mouth, not to mention silver spoon. This shows that no matter the level you are now, even if your condition is very bad, the ideas shared in this book can help you; and that is if you read with an open mind and **get to work**.

Let's get down to business.

P.S You will find one or two grammatical errors in this book. Forgive me, I am a human like you. And, my aim of writing the book in the first place is to communicate with you and not appear grammatically sophisticated. I have also included a little of our local parlance here in Nigeria. This is to make sure you relate well with what I am sharing.

WHAT MANY DON'T KNOW!

There are principles that rule on earth here. Those who know and apply them thrive and maximize their place on earth but those who don't, are always full of frustrations and disappointment which is visible in their pitiable explanations and exasperated demeanor. They are always wondering why things are not working for them like it does for others despite their efforts and "hard work". I have been there. I have blamed the devil countless times that I almost wanted to start blaming God too. It never changed anything, in fact, it got worse. I blamed my village people, yet, nothing changed at all.

It became clearer to me when Pastor Korede Komaiya explained it in a simple statement; "the difference between the success and failure is tapping into the power of conscious minority." The conscious minority knows and practice what others don't. And the result; they get what other don't get.[1]

To this I believe that knowledge advantage is one of the greatest advantage. When one has the right knowledge and this knowledge is cultivated through creative thinking backed by deliberate actions, such a person devices tools that help them eliminate hindrances and achieve their success in a very simple way that almost makes you think "it is really simple". A young man can be born in a poor home and yet enjoy the advantage a person born into affluence cannot enjoy. How can this happen? By knowing what the other doesn't know and doing what the others don't do. In business, relationship, and every works of life, I have realized that this is the difference maker and not just prayer, fasting and anointing as Africans think. This does not mean they are not effective.

What I am about to share with you are simple life secrets. Are they really secrets? Well, I don't think they are. They are simple life hacks and principles that many are blinded to because they are too simple to really mean anything much.

IF ONLY...

If only I can get an opportunity to go for that event, I know my life will change for good.

If only I can get an opportunity to leave this country, I know things will change for me.

If only I can get an opportunity to go to school, my life will be better.

If only I get the opportunity to meet that man, I know he will help me.

These are everyday conversations people have with others and with themselves. Opportunity is one thing everyone is looking for. We all believe that just an opportunity is enough to change our lives. Well, that might be true.

I keep hearing people say. . .I'm just looking for the right opportunity. More often than not, most people aren't looking for an opportunity, they're simply waiting for it to knock on the door and say "here I am." It doesn't work that way. Thomas Edison, the inventor, once said, "Opportunity is missed by most people because it is dressed in overalls and looks like work."

It is the work part that I want to demystify for you my friend. I want to make it easier and help you see how easy it is to enjoy opportunities every single day of your life. I am not ashamed to also share my own experiences and flaws here. I have promised to be very open to you, so you can see how these things work and how you can benefit from them.

Consider this as a *brother helping brother* thing. You must raise your level of expectation, by expecting opportunities to come your way every day. Truth of the matter is, you only need one opportunity -the right one.

It's probably been there all along but you just haven't seen it yet.

Everyone is searching for opportunity. Business men are searching for the next big shift, writers are searching for the next big idea, and entrepreneurs are searching for the opportunity of a lifetime to take them to global platforms. In a country like Nigeria, many are searching for the opportunity of leaving to a country where they believe their lives would be made better.

One thing many who are searching for opportunity don't understand is that opportunity *has a global address and there are protocols to access* opportunity. Yes, there is a protocol to follow. It is not some rules and regulations to follow but principles knitted into life to make things happen at ease. Many are praying, others wishing and hoping. While many struggle and others patiently wait for opportunities, there are those who are busy creating and taking hold of opportunities daily. They enjoy opportunities every single day they wake up. Are they specially gifted or have a certain preference from God above others? Why is this happening? The answer is not hidden. It's right in front of you; they have an *understanding*. I will be sharing all that with you in this book.

What you are about to discover in this book are principles that control the lock of opportunities. If you get them right, you will never beg for opportunity anymore. You will never struggle for it either. You will also learn from this book how you can become a human magnet that attracts open doors. What you will find within the pages of this book will change the way you think and see things, and this will place you in a position where you will be able to prepare for, recognize and seize opportunities at ease.

Just follow me through the pages, something awaits you.

CHAPTER ONE

LIMITING BELIEFS

Most of the things we see as limitations presently, are simply mental programming that found its way into our lives from family, culture, religion, environment, association and unguarded exposure to toxic ideologies or information. Some we made up to accommodate our laziness, bad attitude, and shallow way of viewing life. For some, it's a way of consoling ourselves in our bad condition. And truth is, they sabotage our overall progress. They affect almost every decision we make and ultimately determines the result we get out of life.

These narratives filter our lenses and determines what we see and how we see them. As one man see a cup as half full, the other see same cup as half empty. It all boils down to our mental programming.

This becomes more deadly and dangerous when it has a little dose of religious teachings and biblical verses to back it up. It makes it difficult for a man to truly prosper and enjoy what was designed to be enjoyed in life. Blaming unseen powers and the devil is a normal thing for the average African, who doesn't know that he or she is only yielding results based on their mental programming. **Some people today, are only fighting their reflection**.

We have built within our minds and religious gatherings a certain hate for riches and the rich while poverty and the poor seem to look like a great virtue. It's all about our mindset. While there are "elements" of truth to some of these beliefs, when not used in the proper context, it allows our errors to slip through, making us settle for less; a "just surviving state" of living.

In this chapter, I want to talk about certain mindsets that can hinder a man from accessing opportunities daily. These are negative ideas passed down to us, which has made it difficult for people to walk through great doors and have a better life. And if YOU must get RESULTS out of what I am about to show you in this book, then it is expedient we talk about some of these narratives affecting us as young people.

The longevity of a lie doesn't make it true, I hope you know that. A lie can stay for centuries, yet, that doesn't make it turn into truth automatically. It's still a lie. Over time, I have come to understand that a lot of hindrances we face on this part of the world is not really much about the great enemy of humanity-Satan, but our culture, mindset, the narratives passed down to us. We have refused to let them go as times has changed.

What are these wrong dispositions?

ALL FINGERS ARE NOT EQUAL.

This particular "manage your condition" mindset has made a lot of people massage their poverty, unproductivity and left them to wine with mediocrity.

Even if all fingers are not equal, NO ONE FORCED YOU TO BE THE SMALLEST FINGER. That's a decision you are to make, whether to be the smallest finger or the tallest finger. Remember this is not a call for an unhealthy competition with the man next to you. Your fight is different. It's a fight against the poor condition you were born into. It's a fight against the smallness you came to meet in life. It's a battle of making a difference in the world.

Some of our parents held on to this belief, making it look like there were some people designed to die in poverty while the rest bask in abundance and prosperity. The resources and blessing on earth can go round to every living being on earth, so there is no way you can tell me that some people were born to die small.

Yes all fingers are not equal but no one declared you the smallest finger. You need to start seeing beyond where you are now. You can be a great success without obstructing the greatness of another.

YOU CAN BE MORE. Your prosperity and success will not stop the success of another man. Why remain small when you can be big and not interrupt the "bigness" of another person. Since your success cannot stop the success of another man, that means we all can be tall without obstructing another man's tallness. Choose to be tall. Tall financially, tall in terms of result, impact, relevance, influence and all round. If you remain small, it's your choice.

Stop telling yourself that all fingers are not equal. That mindsets comforts poverty and mediocrity. It's a massage therapy for smallness in life. It makes you comfortable in not having and achieving maximum impact and result.

A PATIENT DOG EATS THE FATEST BONE

First my friend, you are not a dog.

Secondly, why must dog always eat bone? Will the world end because a dog ate meat?

Thirdly, a bone is still a bone no matter how fat it is. Poverty is poverty even if you wear it a coat of many colours. Suffering is suffering no matter the bible verse you use to console yourself.

This is one mindset that makes most people STAY IN POVERTY AND UNPRODUCTIVITY for the rest of their life, thinking they are being spiritual and they are practicing patience as a virtue. That's not patient because you are not a dog, a dog must not always eat bone and no matter how fat a bone is, it's still a bone.

Nothing moves until you move. Your life will not move no matter how many hours you pray if all you do is pray. There is no one anywhere whose **life assignment** is to sit and think of how to make you progress in life.

Did you get that?

I repeat, your life will never move no matter how you pray, if all you do is pray and not act. Prayer is not for God to endorse your irresponsibility. Because you can't use prayer to make Him do what he has given you the power to do.

My friend, you need to change some of these things you use to comfort yourself for not having visible results. Some will tell you to take things easy. No! let me tell you, nothing wonderful is ever gained by taking it easy. It requires a dogged commitment on your path.

Hold it there my friend.

What will be will not be. You know why?

Life doesn't happen by chance. It doesn't happen by luck, it happens by choice.

Good thing will not just happen, they will be made to happen by someone. What will be, will not be just like that. Someone has to make something happen.

I will boldly tell you that **what will be, will only be, if you do what you need to do to make it be**. (Remember I told you that I will break grammatical rules)

Yes, every married woman can give birth someday, but it won't happen by itself. Her husband must take a deliberate step to have sex with her to make a baby. Life doesn't regulate itself. Things are made to happen. Many have been living with this ideology, leaving their life to chance.

A man said to me one day "The birds of the air doesn't sow, yet they reap and enjoy plenty, so relax good things will come to you someday." And immediately I replied him…. **Remember the birds of the air, doesn't sit in their nest to enjoy the plenty… they fly out every day. So you have to fly out of your couch too.**

God only bless the works of our hands not our butts on the couch. That is why there is nothing like anointing for laziness.

No matter your fasting and prayer, if you don't take actions, nothing moves. So stop dwelling on "what will be will be…. This will make you live at the mercy of whatever life throws at you.

My friend, you can decide your fate.

Don't leave your life in the hands of chance. That guy will mess it up and in the end, you will blame *village people.*

ONE DAY E GO BETTER (IT WILL BE OK ONE DAY)

I grew up in an average Nigerian home. My parents were able to provide what we needed; at least the basic things humans need to survive. Even though it was a bit comfortable for us then, everything changed when I lost my mum. She was the person who provided more in the home.

My dad wasn't really following financial principles that could make money multiply, so even though he was earning, it wasn't long enough several things set in and things began to fall apart drastically. We struggled through and I entered the university. My pre-degree program and part of my first year didn't come with much financial stress. But in the second semester, it was obvious I might not graduate due to financial challenges.

Miraculously, I was able to pull through my first year. I kept telling myself that things will get better someday. We moved from living in a comfortable house to living in a one room apartment in Port Harcourt (Nigeria) and my siblings had to be taken to the village. This was almost unbearable. Yet, I kept telling myself, "one day everything will be fine". I did nothing but just hope that one day things will get better. I moved to my second year, paying fees became a challenge. I missed the first semester exams and at that time, I knew everything is finished. I stepped down for a year but miraculously, I was called to lead in the campus fellowship. After sharing my story with some of the leaders, they were able to help me the next year first semester.

Along the line I had to sit with myself and have a one on one conversation with myself. That was when I decided that I will do everything possible to graduate no matter what. At that point I met Collins Eromosole, who introduced me to a business. We buy refurbished blackberry phones in Onitsha (Anambra State, Nigeria) and sell in school. I could buy a phone for N25,000 and sell it for N35,000 – N40,000 in school. I remember my first profit was about N12,000. That was when my eyes opened. I knew if things would change, then I've got work to do.

The phone business didn't survive up to a semester as the school authority didn't allow the use of camera phones. I switched to Selling clothes in school. I would go to Onitsha and buy a dozens of nice shirts for N10,000 and sell. I could sell a pair of shirt for N2,000. This particular business really went well as it helped me survive in school as well as raise a little portion to support my school fees because my people at the fellowship were there to support me with loan to complete the fees. After exams, I still continued my business to repay back the borrowed part of my fees.

Sometimes business was very bad, but there were times it went well too.

At this point, I already stopped going home for unnecessary breaks. I asked myself "of what use is going back home to meet the same condition that will leave me depressed. I was never happy going for holidays because of the condition back at home. I began to learn how to live away from home during holidays. To make matters worse, my dad fell seriously ill at a time. So, I had to also support from the little I earned in my small hustle.

But I am glad that one single decision helped me take a stand and a step which resulted to me being a university graduate today.

You see, a lot of us console ourselves, and also shy away from making tough and difficult decisions or taking risk that will propel us forward because of this mindset; **"one day e go better"**. We just believe everything is in God's hands. And when it pleases God, He will come down from His throne of glory and settle the matter for us.

My friend, it doesn't work that way.

It will not please God in the next two years to bail you out of poverty. Your poverty has displeased him already and that's why he has sent Jesus to die. That's why he gave His spirit. That's why he has empowered everyone with great gifts and abilities.

If you are the type that believes one day it will be fine and just sit there waiting for that one miraculous and glorious day, it will never come.

Yes, you have been motivated, you were told that everything will be fine tomorrow. Sorry to spoil your theology, many people have waited for a tomorrow that is better than today and never saw it. Having a better tomorrow begins with doing today, things that will propel you into a better reality tomorrow.

If you want things to get better one day, then start today making conscious decisions and taking deliberate steps. Today is the beginning of that one day.

Tomorrow starts today.

The future you are looking for is in the decisions you make today. The future doesn't just happen because it has been scripted down, but because someone took deliberate steps to make the script become a reality.

Time flies even when you are not conscious of it. It's just like people say, "time waits for no man." Tomorrow will certainly come. That future you heard about yesterday will certainly arrive. But the big question is "can the future design itself in your favour?"

The future is a cumulative result of the choices made yesterday and today. Tomorrow is only a fruit of the seed sown today. You can't reap a better tomorrow if you don't sow a good seed today.

Tomorrow has no power to design itself in your favour. It only takes the shape of the consequences of your actions and inactions today. Since the future cannot design itself, why not start now by giving it that perfect shape and look you desire. The resources have been made available by God. All that is left for you to do is, BUILD.

I am not an advocate of jumping the process of greatness. I am not encouraging impatience. I am not discouraging "days of little beginning," but I have few questions to ask.

When is God's time to bless you?

When is God's time to take you out of poverty?

When is God's time to move you from that poor living condition you are in right now?

When is God's time for you to have access to three square meals?

When is God's time to make you stop living from hand to mouth?

When is God's time to make at least one person in your family a person of influence?

When is God's time to give you that business opportunity and breakthrough you have been asking for in years now?

If you know God's time for any of these questions, just drop the book and wait for that time. You don't need to read further.

OPPORTUNITY COMES BUT ONCE

Blessed be the Lord, who daily loadeth us with benefits, even the God of our salvation. Selah.[2]

Opportunities walk pass us every single day of our lives. The problem is not with the unavailability of opportunities but with inability of the man to see. Can your eyes really see?

Every day comes with its own unique opportunities and if you fall for the lie that it only comes once in a life time, even when they come, your mind can't recognize them.

When I hear that "God's mercies are new every morning," that thought leaves me expectant. It leaves me with confidence and assurance knowing that if God shows me mercy every new day, his mercy brings favour that day and opportunities are just part of such favour. Opportunities comes every day we are alive. It only takes empowered minds and trained eyes to see and lay hold of them. In the bus while you commute to work, there is opportunity. In the games, there is. In church, seminars, even weddings, there are opportunities. Little wonder Temple Nwoke in his book Jacob's Porridge said, "There are so many business opportunities on the golf course more than the board room."[3]

Good things were not designed to come to us once in our life time. Open doors and breakthrough are not one time events. They happen daily. We only need to understand certain life principles that make them a reality.

THERE IS NO SPECIAL DAY.

Opportunity does not have a time keeper.

If it's not your time, opportunity will not come. This is one thing I have heard from people a lot of times. Some even try to use some sort of unbalanced religious ideologies to support this, claiming that God has a specific day to bless you and as long as that day has not come, you will continue to suffer till it's your day. EVERY DAY IS SPECIAL. If you don't identify those things that makes it special, you will keep living each day waiting for the miraculous day of glory when things will happen for you.

Every day is opportunity day.

Every single day is the same but it is the events that happens in each of the days that redefines it for us. Opportunity doesn't have a specific day of the week or month of the year it comes out of its shell and start looking for whom to change their lives. It can come any day and any time. It's just like saying God has specific days he answers prayers and every other day, he turns deaf ears to prayers.

Opportunity does not have a special day. You have to be rightly positioned to recognize and grab it any day when it walks pass you. And it doesn't often come with sirens or convoy. You need a trained mind to recognize it.

I have often said that, God's readiness to bless you is dependent upon your readiness to be blessed not based on what your calendar says. The moment you get yourself to fully believe this, your eyes will open to the opportunities around you.

Every day can be your day. Even while you are reading this, it can come knocking at your door but if you don't have a resourceful mind, it will pass you while you continue to look for it, hoping that God decides to smile on you someday.

Opportunity has a global address.

To **make opportunities come to you**, then you ought to understand that opportunity has a global address. It simply means that opportunity lives everywhere. It has a residential address in Nigeria, Africa, Asia, North America, Australia, Europe and anywhere you can think of.

Don't put a limitation on your breakthrough.

CHAPTER TWO

TODAY IS THE DAY

Keep your expectation in front of you every morning when you wake up. It makes it easier for you to recognize opportunities that leads you to them.

Many people pray, God hears and send answers. But somehow, this answers don't get to the people who have asked. Sometimes it seems like the mail man from heaven missed the address. No, he didn't. The problem is that Often times, we fail to recognize the answer when it comes. Because the answer wears something different from the picture in our minds.

Praying for something, and recognizing that thing when it arrives are two different things. This is the reason for so many delayed breakthrough and miracles. Some people who don't understand this blame the devil for delaying their breakthrough and destiny. Some accuse their relatives for being responsible for the delayed answers and so many other things.

If you are praying for rain, then make sure you carry your umbrella as you step out. If you preparing for an opportunity, then go out every day ready to grab it.

Inability to recognize opportunities is the major challenge.

Opportunities don't come with an entourage neither does it come with a siren. So you need a resourceful mind to see it, and part of the way of seeing it, is preparing everyday to receive the opportunity. When you wake up every day, move into the day with full conviction that you will get the life-time opportunity you have been seeking for. Hal Elrod in his book *The Miracle Equation* said, "You are only two decisions away from everything you want; Unwavering faith and extraordinary effort."

Your unwavering faith and expectation affects your mental positioning which in turn affects everything you do for that day.

Your thoughts creates your reality. When you mentally position yourself for opportunities, here is what it will do for you;

- It will affect the way you act. This will help modify the way you behave that day. It leaves you prepared always.

Attitude is a very important factor in this equation.

- It will affect how you relate with people that day. Opportunities comes through people. **People are couriers that deliver opportunities**. And if you learn how to relate with people, manage relationships, then those opportunities can come even from strangers.
- It will affect how you respond to things, news, people, words, situations and lots more. Perception changes everything.

Perception is powerful. Your reactions to things, news, events, and even people's attitude towards you can be greatly and positively influenced when you live with a sense of readiness that your opportunity can come today. It helps you redefine situations, knowing that often times the opportunities can come but will not be wearing a shining gold apparel but a garment disguised as problems and challenges.

- It will affect your decision for the day. You are one decision away from something great happening in your life. Living with that sense of readiness helps to positively affect the decisions you make every day.

All these help you walk ready. It puts you in the mental state of identifying platforms or chances that will bring about a big testimony or opening for you. If you cannot prepare for it in your heart and mind daily, you might never have it. Some people believe that their opportunity will come in one particular distant day. No, it can come now. If you treat today as your day of opportunity, it will change you; your actions will be affected and you find yourself navigating towards open doors.

Seeing everyday as your day of breakthrough changes the way you think, your attitudes and behaviours and makes you a ready magnet for open doors.

Move from being opportunity-hopeful to opportunity-ready.

Wake up each day declaring to yourself and to the world that you are walking into that thing you have prayed or wished for. Tell yourself that you are already walking in the reality of it. Nothing pulls things into realization like powerful word spoken by a man whose spirit is convinced, a man whose heart is full of faith.

CHAPTER THREE

JUST ONE THING

Treat people, performance, business, relationship, and situation as the doorway to your greatness because, they truly are.

If you understand human behavior and the principles that govern good relationships, attracting the best opportunities becomes easy.

You are one person away from your breakthrough.

You are one decision away from your expectations.

You are one project away from the million dollar contract you desire.

You are one conversation away from the circle that will place you on the stage of the big players in your industry.

You are one performance away from your record deal.

Give a client your best even though they didn't pay for such, not because of them but another person who would see the good work and need your services.

Every job well done is an open door for more clients. Every client is a potential door to your next big win in business. Thread wisely.

Every job excellently done is an open door to accessing more clients. Do every Job like it's the job that will launch you into that dream contract. By so doing, **you are at your best always** and that brings opportunities without you going to look for it. When jobs are badly done, it tells badly of the person who did it. It makes it difficult to be sought after, or recommended. This idea I am sharing might not sound too cool with the present ideologies gotten out there, but it does pay. It makes you an opportunity magnet. It is the law of value.

People are couriers that deliver opportunities.

Behind opportunities are men.

Sometime in April 2019, I was at home and all of a sudden, I got a notification on my phone. It was a message from Mrs. Divine Eze, a first time author. She was ready to publish her book, and was in need of someone to edit her manuscript and design the layout. I was recommended for the job.

As we conversed, she opened up that she could not afford the amount I was charging then. I asked how much she was able to provide to help edit her book. She said N15, 000. 15,000? My eyes were wide open as that was too little compared to the magnitude of the job to be done for her. She pleaded and I understood with her. So I took on the job and decided to do it. I had different thoughts running through my head. I thought of doing everything shabbily because of the size of the pay. But after careful thought, it dawned on me that this particular job might be my door to the breakthrough I seek.

I gave it my best. After the job, this lady wrote me the best review I can ever think of. (see image below) Boom! Calls and messages reached me from different places. Just on the day she posted that review on her Facebook timeline, I got 5 new clients to work with. After that, few months later, I kept getting new people who always said to me, "We saw Divine Eze's post about you and decided to reach so you can help us with our book work".

A single job well done for Mrs. Divine Eze got me to work for Oti Bolarinwa, and Mr. Gerald Nwadike. And this led to many other jobs. It didn't just stop there, she went ahead to recommend me to her clients.

I have consistently been practicing this and it keeps working for me. I have met some people who run successful online business and this happens to be one of their "trade secrets." Haven worked online for a while now, I can say I've gotten more jobs from referrals than running an advert. Once a client is happy with your job, he/she will easily sell your services to others who need it. It saves you the stress you have to go through trying to convince a new client. And that is more money for you and more doors opening. Now don't get me wrong, I am not trying to say that you have to sell your services cheap because you need to magnet opportunities and to work with more clients. All I am saying is that sometimes, you have to look pass your present economics and do certain things to position yourself in the future for something worth more than what you are getting now. I am simply saying don't look down on any client. They are the reason you are in business.

Back to business!

5 Million Naira Lost

A young man lost a business opportunity that would have given him 5 million Naira. Here is how everything happened.

He has been in the business of supplying electronics, hardware and other computer parts. He is good at what he does but there was one problem; Nnamdi always had a story to tell about people's money. In December 2015 he did a business with a woman at Nyanya (Abuja, Nigeria) and he didn't finish delivering the goods. According to him, his brother fell ill and all his money were used up in trying to save his life. But one mistake he made was not picking the woman's call and oftentimes rejecting it.

The woman who wanted these things for the new school her husband opened for her got fed up and decided to let go.

In July 2018, Nnamdi got a call from a friend and he was linked to a wealthy politician in Abuja who needed computers and television for his new hotels. He submitted his quotation and was asked to come get his first payment for the deal. While he was still chatting with the man waiting for the cheque to be signed and given to him, a woman walked into the office.

Guess who she was.

The woman who Nnamdi has been dodging. She is the wife of the man who was supposed to give him a cheque. That business was terminated immediately and was even asked to bring the N250,000 he made away with or face the consequences. When he narrated his story, i felt sorry for him but, it served as a lesson for me.

It takes just one thing to gain access to that place you have always dreamt of.

You see, it has always been said "you can do whatever you like, you are free, but being free from the consequences of your action is not a guarantee". Sincerity and integrity are not just some sort of Christian virtues that will make you go to heaven. It is the bedrock of long lasting relationship, and lasting business. If you can develop it, you will become an opportunity magnet. Emeka Nobis in His book "Four Feet Five" emphasized on this a lot; sincerity and integrity.

There are many talented people out there, but the world has gone pass the time they look up to talented people. They are looking for people with reputable character to do business with. This is why I have always said that integrity can serve as a capital for your business. (That's a lesson for another day.)

You can be gifted, eloquent, but if you lack integrity, it will be difficult to have opportunities come to you.

This sounds like I am preaching morals now. No I am not. I am simply sharing with you facts of life we young people seldom ignore in this present day where everyone just wants to be a lion to devour the next gazelle they see. Words like this might not mean much to a lot of people out there especially in this season where money is respected more than character. I have been trapped by these same things, but I have grown. Now I know better, and I am better at doing business. Integrity pays in high currencies.

MASTER HUMAN RELATIONSHIP

Behind every opportunity is a man. Don't go spiritual on me now my friend. I know you might be thinking, "It's God that brought it." Yes you are right, but GOD USED A MAN.

Humans are couriers of opportunities.

You can never have access to opportunities in isolation. You need human connections. Connecting with other people makes for a better life said Rabbi Daniel Lapin in his book *Business secrets from the Bible*. This is one law that is inextricable from the natural world. Trying to conquer the world while remaining isolated from others is as futile as all other attempts to defy nature's law. God wants us to connect with one another. And to maintain connections that brings opportunities at ease, you must master human relationship.

First you need to understand that no matter how gifted you are, the potential you carry, Productivity and fruitfulness in life endeavors goes beyond hard work. Relationship is a key factor, and understanding how to relate with people will enable you harness the benefits. If you must become the kind of person that attracts opportunities, you must do away with the "self-made" ideology. Is any man in this life really self-made? My friend, you need people. Forget all these jargons and bragging you hear from some musicians. "…. I came from the streets… I am a self-made millionaire." That's codeine and Tramadol speaking. (Google that) There are fans who promoted their works, shared their links, videos, post about them, and bought tickets to their shows. There were crews that supported them, producers who had many sleepless night trying to mix the best beats ever. And now you say you are self-made? My guy,

Shut Up!

Even if you don't know how to do anything else in life but understand the dynamics of relationships, you will enjoy opportunities at ease. There are people you must meet in life to make a hit. And even when you meet them and don't have human relation skills, you will lose out. Your greatest opportunities will come either through participation, cooperation or partnership with at least one person or another. This is how life was designed to function.

Opportunity come all the time. But if you are only concerned about your stomach, you will miss out. If you want to be someone who attracts opportunities at ease, your economics must not be priority. What you do will not impact your essence or meaning as an individual if it is only motivated by your economics. (By economics I mean, what to eat, drink or wear)

Over deliver.

If you are a writer, artist or public speaker, every platform you climb and every time you are opportune to speak, **over deliver.**

In the words of Salem King, "**Anything worth doing is worth over doing.**" (Tweet that!) For me, being paid cash is the lowest form of reward for my labour. I strive to do jobs that brings me not just cash but recommendations and open doors. This is real reward for me. I choose to be paid for both my time and the result I achieve on a project. I believe the best way to be paid for the result achieved on a project is **cash plus recommendation**. You should try that.

Again, I say over deliver.

It's not just about that event alone. You don't know everyone seated in that auditorium. Even if you do, you don't know where your tapes will get to; especially in this digital age. You are just one platform away from THE PLATFORM. You are just one business away from THE BUSINESS. You are just one client away from THE CLIENT.

This is one sure way of accessing opportunities easily. I travel a lot, to speak in churches and seminars. There are some churches this year alone I have gone to more than 4 times. Not because I am the best they can have; "over delivery" is my secret.

I have been to meetings, seminars, church conferences with not more than 10 -15 people in attendance. But if you see me preparing for such meeting, you would think I was getting set to appear in a world Presidents Forum.

No audience is small. No platform is small. Don't say because they are just starters and may be 12 in number you just speak shabbily and then walk away.

Or maybe they didn't wear designer clothes and bags to the events so you assume "these ones are not the kind of "big" shots I am looking for." Don't use packaging to deceive yourself and deny yourself of open doors. I know you are trying not to appear cheap. I get that. You are not cheap, but you still must know, the size of the crowd doesn't reflect the size of the returns.

My friend, No gathering is small.

If 12 is enough for Jesus, even 5 can open doors for you. Within those few people seated are world changers, great people who don't carry their portfolios on their forehead. You need to be wise. Wisdom is a factor that will help you stand out when others are begging to have some things. Prepare like you have never done before, and deliver maximally. This kind of personal attitude keeps you at your best always.

Treat people like they are your door way to your greatest desire, because they are. People are very important as far as your lifting is concerned. If you don't have money, you have not lost all. But if you don't have the skills to treat people right, you might lose all. Because even God bless men through people, places, and situations. Lot was blessed through a man,

Abraham. Joseph was remembered by a man. David was recommended by a man. Nehemiah received help from God through a man. Mankind received help from God through a man; Christ. The widow of Zarephat received help from God through a man-Elijah. Elijah in turn received help from God through a widow. The Shunamite woman received help through a man-Elisha. Don't play with relationship. Men are your access and key. Men are couriers of opportunities.

Don't do a bad job because a client paid less. Your reputation is hanging on every job you do.

I learnt this after losing great clients and my business suffered; and my pocket suffered too. Don't mess with the job in your hands right now. It can open and shut doors. That video you are about to shoot now, give it your best. Deliver excellent Jobs, your "breakthrough" client just needs to see that excellent work and give you a call that will change your life. This might not make sense to my super spiritual brothers and sisters who feel God is obligated to lift them because they fasted and prayed. But these are simple life principles that help you stand out when others are begging for a position.

My friend, these things work like a chain. They are connected.

Collaborate.

Don't live a competitive life. No one is your competition. Collaboration is the new competition. I have always believed that your life's success is tied to your responsibility to see other lives succeed. It is very important for you to be actively involved with other people. There's so much to be gained by cooperative friendship and productive collaboration.

Stop trying to conquer the world alone. You will suffer man. Opportunity comes to people who understand the power of synergy. I have found repeatedly, when one seeks to raise his own life and business apart from others, he tends to fail. On the other hand, when you seek to raise others, you succeed and enjoy opportunities. Because your life is a part of a greater whole.

Before we move to the next chapter, let me leave you with the words of Melissa Eisler,

"Create good Karma- As much as creating opportunities is based on doing, it's also about how you do it. Being a good person and putting positivity into the Universe invites good things to happen in return. **Take time to genuinely connect with others, instead of having a one-track mind for building an opportunity for yourself. By creating lasting, solid relationships, people will remember you when an opportunity arises that requires your expertise. And when and where you can, volunteer your time and talent! Offer guidance and counsel based on your skills, establishing credibility and laying the foundation for when a full-blown opportunity presents itself.** If you have a listening ear and want to become a counselor, volunteer your services at a local community center or offer your time pro bono at a counseling firm. Even if an opportunity doesn't manifest immediately, have faith that something is on the horizon.

I hope you are beginning to see how these things work?

Let's move to the next point where I will show you another important factor in the opportunity equation.

CHAPTER FOUR

CREATE SOLUTIONS

Problems are opportunities waiting to be maximized.

A young man who was desperate about getting wealthy heard of a wise old man living in the village next to his. He was told that anyone who goes to the man becomes rich, so he set out to meet this great man.

He set out, and after a day's journey he arrived at the village. It was pretty easy for him to locate the old man in question. When he arrived, the old man inquired to find out why he was sought after.

"I have heard that many people who come to you get rich. I also want to be rich" he said.

"I see," the old man replied.

"You will live with me for one week and if you are able to accomplish the task i have for you within that period of time, then you will be rich and also free to go back to where you came from".

The next day, the old man came back from the bush and handed over to the young man a lump that looked like a big rock covered with earth. The old man said, help me find the gold in this.

'The young man looked at the dirty thing covered with hard soil and said, "How do you think there can be gold in this?"

The old man simply replied, "find me the gold inside".

The young man stood there wondering how he would go about the task. He doesn't seem to understand why he would be given an earth covered rock to find gold inside when he actually came to be shown the way to riches.

The first day passed, he still couldn't find a way to remove lump of earth covering the "supposed" gold. All he did was stare at the rock all day. When the old man came back and saw him sitting down in front of the lump of soil, he smiled and walked away.

This continued for two days and on the third night, an idea came to the young man. "Why not try using water," he said to himself.

The next morning, He got a big jar, filled with water and dropped the lump of earth inside. He sat there patiently waiting and gradually, the earth began to dissolve away. Within 30 minutes, it all dissolved and there it was "A shiny little object."

Immediately, the young man took the stone and ran to the old man "i did it" he said. I found the treasure. The old man smiled and said to him, "sit down my son".

"When i gave you this task, you felt it was impossible, the lump didn't look like anything good. I believe you must have thought you were wasting your time and wondering if there would be treasure in this. And more importantly, how can this help you get rich.

It was a problem to you the first day i gave it to you, but somehow, you were able to solve it and get the treasure out.

Getting rich follows the same process, my son.

Look well at the community where you are coming from, there are many treasures laying around, but you can't see them. You know why? Because they are within a lump of earth- things that look like a problem to you and others. Inside these problems are your wealth.

The same way you came up with a way to remove this earth and got me this treasure, if you can create solutions to solve those problems that are around you, inside them you will find the treasures that will make you wealthy beyond your imagination".

BE A SOLUTION PROVIDER

A lot of us in this part of the world have been indoctrinated with the wrong perception or idea about problems. We have been taught to run away from problems. If things get tough, the first idea is to run. We are always told to stay away from problems and be careful. Religion teaches us to fast and pray endlessly against problems and possibly any man or woman that will bring problems our way. We are taught to depend on God to give us solutions to our problems. That's faith right? I don't think so. We have been taught to sow seeds against problems and do anything possible to make sure problems stay far away from us.

We don't want to be associated with anything or environment that there is problem. And that is why some are running away from our country today. They believe that when they run to other countries, they won't find problems there. One thing we don't understand is that problems are blessings in disguise. Pastor Segun Obadje in *The Leverage* devotional said, "The mistake people make is, they look for opportunities with the label 'opportunity' on them. Opportunities don't carry labels with their exact names on them; they carry labels of problems, crises, challenges, and confusions." But within them are the opportunities you seek.

In the words of Sunday Adelaja "where there is problem, there is money."[4] Permit me to also say, *where there is problem, there is opportunity for anyone willing to create solution.* Opportunities can arise from bad situations if you are willing to learn from it, and engage in creative thinking to create a solution. Problems are opportunities waiting to be maximized. Problems are opportunities in work clothes. There are many opportunities out there for us all. Many young people don't have what it takes to recognize it. Even when we see one, our cultural and religious mental programming redefines the picture and scares us away from it.

See, where there is problem, there is money. Where there is problem there are opportunities. Anyone who brings solution to the table is the one who goes with the money. I tell my students in our quarterly writer's trainings, **where there is a problem, there should be a book with the solutions. And when there is a book with solutions, there is money for the author of the book with the solutions**.

Problems and opportunities have a cordial relationship. "We all detest problems, but problems are the reason for every improvement we make. Problems quickens your wit. Problems stiffens your spine. Problems force you to think outside the box. A problem is an opportunity to step into a new dimension of accomplishment."[5] Problems makes us inventors, they help us express our creativity.

When opportunities arise, men don't look for takers, they look for givers. Men don't look for people who have nothing to bring to the table. **Creating solutions to problems positions you as a go to person when there is a need.** Look at the life of the biblical David. Even if he was never anointed to be king over the people of Israel, and eventually opportunity shows up, he would be elected to be king of Israel. You know why? He solved a national problem and that put him on the spotlight. When you solve problem as big as goliath, you become someone whose identity cannot be hidden. Opportunity seeks to embrace solution providers.

Imagine that you have two young men living under you, one is your biological son, and the other, your slave. Whenever there are issues or challenges, the slave gets up and solves them even before you are notified and your son sit and do nothing even though of a fact, papers and certificates proves that he can solve such a problem. Now, when you have an opening for a bigger task, who do you think is more capable to handle that for you? A man with certificate and no track record of solved problems or someone without certifications from schools yet has proved to be capable of dealing with such; with enough records and evidence. A careful look at this will give you an insight why a lot of prayerful and tongue talking Christians don't step into bigger platforms and yet people who you think are not or even less spiritual enjoy massive opportunities. Without understanding, one will think God is partial or doesn't listen to prayers. This is the same reason why talented people are hungry yet, people with "little or none" make news all the time. It's simple. Show up and do it even when everyone is running away from it.

Here is one thing most young people in our generation don't understand. They are always looking for where to take from. They don't like doing free services. If it will not bring something for them, then they have no part in it. Now you see why many are struggling to climb to the top. I am not saying you should go about doing business for free. But there will be a point in your life when your next level will be dependent upon that. A typical example is when you are still getting started. Learn to offer solutions for free. Do jobs for free. At this point, you don't have the connections or the name to attract that opportunities to yourself. Your option would be to grow your network. Remember that people are couriers that deliver opportunities. And one way to grow your network is giving solution to people. This are the very people who will put in words for you and make the opportunities come running to you. One great thing about this is that, no one will force you to do free jobs for them, you are the one who gets to decide who you will provide solution for.

Learn to offer service as a way of contributing to humanity, society or community. You mustn't get cash out of every little help you render. For me, I have always believed that being paid cash of the lowest form of payment. Don't get me wrong, I still like to be paid cash too.

You can also see this kind of mindset in the way most of our young people relate with the "rich" in the society. They believe the rich must be taken from. Anytime they find themselves around wealthy people, all they are thinking is how to milk the person dry, not what or how to add to this person. One thing many fail to understand is that even the rich have challenges and sometimes need help.

There are opportunities that I have enjoyed that came just by solving problems for free. Everything is not about money. But don't let anyone bully you into thinking that you are being inconsiderate for charging a fee for a solution you are bringing to the table. Please remember money is important.

The principle of creating solutions makes us look pass our present day need and position ourselves for the future. As someone who has been in the internet space for a little while now, I can tell you this principle works. Sometimes when certain influencers want to sell their books, courses or programs and give out commission to people, I take part and reject the commission. I tell them directly that I prefer a relationship with them than the 2k commission I will get. Sometimes I have gone ahead to design their book covers and e-books or event flyers for free. I have gotten a lot of clients through their recommendations too. You have to understand that, no effort which we extend to those who are in distress can go without some form of adequate reward. Not always does the reward come from those to whom the service is rendered, but it will come from one source or another.

It has worked for me. I mean too many times.

When you have an opportunity, please do things for people. Sends out good karma. What I am trying to say is this; learn to solve problems in the capacity you can. When you see problems in your surrounding or community, while others are running, create a solution. While others are trying to leave the country because of the many problems rocking it, stay put and think of a solution. With that, you can make a whole nation become your paying client. That is one way to position yourself for lifting.

Africa is one of the richest continent on earth. Not because of her numerous mineral resources but because of her numerous problems yet to be solved. Those are wealth untapped. Those are opportunities waiting to be maximized.

Remember that opportunity doesn't come with siren. It won't even look like it most times. But only those who have trained themselves would recognize it. Stop running from problems. Some people will think you are foolish for running towards a problem everyone is running away from. You can't blame them for thinking that way.

They see problems, you see opportunities.

CHAPTER FIVE

CREATIVE THINKING

Do you know you can create opportunities?

Yes!

Opportunities can be created.

The question is how? It's pretty simple; thinking.

Not just thinking, but **Creative Thinking**.

Many of us young Africans are beginning to understand the importance of reading. We are now beginning to see that it is not just something to do because of some tests and examinations we must pass. It exposes us to knowledge, but more important is the cultivation of this knowledge. This is what creative thinking is; cultivation of knowledge.

Reading is like acquiring a piece lands. And the only time the lands yields fruits is when they are cultivated. This is what thinking does for us. Our minds has been designed with an intrinsic ability to create things; and opportunity is one of such things.

In this age, as a young person, if you want to magnet opportunities you must engage in creative thinking. And to do this, you must value solitude. In the era of noise, notifications and instant messages, you must make out time to separate yourself and engage in a thinking exercise. This is how to create opportunities out of nothing.

In business and life generally, excessive busyness is corrosive to reflection which in turn inhibits creativity, the well spring of breakthrough ideas and sustainable leadership. Clarity and creativity don't flow in a noisy mind. They come into a mind quieted from distractions.

Don't just be committed to knowing; be more committed to the cultivation of such knowledge into tools and blueprints for results. The mind sees through thinking. According to Samson Adah Paul, "thinking is the eyes of the mind." Knowledge is the raw material for creative thinking. The challenge is that many young people are not "thinking". We don't want to be alone, we don't enjoy solitude. We prefer to be swallowed up by the noise out there; evangelize the latest trend on social media and all that. This is why many are depressed if they are not getting approval from the public via their contents online.

You can create opportunities for yourself if you can sit down and think. No matter how limited your present resource is, creative thinking can open up new ways for you. Little wonder Dr. David Oyedepo once said, if you can think, then what you have is enough. School is not enough. You need to grow to a level where you can sit and cultivate the knowledge passed to you in school to create things; create opportunities not just for yourself but others too.

Many young people today believe that government is responsible for their predicament; inability to make money, marry, have a job, eat good food etc. But it's not true.

Bad news Alert!

God never designed your life to be run by the government.

Creative thinking can help you conquer the embargos that would want to impede your progress. When I say creative thinking, I am talking about **generating tools for eliminating present and potential hindrances to the realization of our dreams and ideas** as young Africans. As you engage in creative thinking, you come up with ways to eliminate excuses and shine your light for the world to see.

Let me share an experience with you. I have been writing books for a while now. Few years ago, my greatest challenge has been how to raise fund to print my books. (I didn't really know much about e-books at that time) But one day, trying to observe my usual time of "aloneness," an idea came. I said to myself, I know how to format a book using two different software, I have little knowledge on graphics design. If I can come up with something, and then save up to buy a small printer, I can actually print my books in small quantity, or in batches (at least for that time till things get better financially). After printing I can take my books out get someone to bind them for me at a low cost.

My friend, it worked. That helped me get started. But thank God things have changed now.

In the words of Ekpo Victor Bassey, "Opportunity is a function of awareness." And I dare say that, thinking breeds awareness and advancement. Thinking activates. Don't just read, think too.

Here is an excerpt from Samson Adah Paul's book *Atomic Knowledge;*

Thinking is not a process of engaging the mind to be conscious of a matter. Thinking is a process of engaging the mind to discover the undiscovered of a matter. Thinking is not engaging a matter to mental consciousness; thinking rather is engaging a matter to mental interrogation, to mental fellowship, to mental intercourse, to mental auditing, to mental examination, and mental debate.[6]

There is so much thinking can do for you. It is strategically moving yourself out of the crowded water of excuses that many find themselves and setting yourself up for opportunities and success.

Creative thinking will help you identify treasure in a garbage. It will help you create opportunities instead of waiting for one. And more importantly, it helps you transform the ordinary into extra ordinary.

If you want to make opportunities come to you, start thinking.

CHAPTER SIX

INTENTIONAL GROWTH

There are doors that will never open for you until you grow into the man who is capable of standing behind such doors; grow.

For many people, a university degree is enough to get them a great life. But degrees don't bring opportunities. Well, it might get you a job. For many others, after going through the university, they see no need why they should waste their valuable time to read books, go for courses, and invest in mentorship programs. Such things are a waste of money for them. Truth is, this is one of the many things that bring you close to your dreams.

A lot of times, we are advised to focus on our goals and that is the way to achieve them. But time has afforded me the experience and wisdom to know that just focusing goals is not enough to make most things in our life happen. Fact is, **the person who sets the goal is different from the person who achieves the goal**.

This simply means that just setting goals is not enough to reach the place you envision. You would have to grow into a different person entirely. This has to happen all round. You would grow in strength, ability to withstand temporary setbacks and bounce back, ability to relate with people better, ability to understand human behaviours, how to network, your leadership capacity and so many others. Permit me to say that **a person who achieves a goals is the better version of the person who set the goals**. Growth is the door that separate the two. Improvement is one of the curtain that separates you from the last little money you were paid and the bigger pay you will receive from the same kind of job. You have to understand that **opportunity lives next door to self-improvement**.

Even scripturally, Paul made it clear that there are things he would not be able to share with his followers, not because they were not entitled to such deep insights, but because they are still babies in their thinking. He went further to also elaborate this using inheritance as an example. As longs as a person is still a child, even though he is entitled to whatever his parents left, he will not access them until he grows (Galatians 4:1-4). Don't underestimate the power of intentional growth.

You don't just start a business and then within a twinkle of an eye, you are cashing out millions from the bank. Well, that's what entrepreneurship looks like in the mind of a person until they start. Even those in the church circle has not really done well in balancing teachings like this. Most of us are made to believe that the moment we start, "anointing" comes upon our business and we start cashing out with money bags. When the opposite becomes our reality, we tend to doubt what we had believed in previously, it throws us into worry and depression.

Look, as the business owner, you will have to grow for certain doors to open up for your business. **Your business growth is also tied to your personal**

growth. I have been in the publishing industry for over 6 years now. When I started, I was wondering when I would be opportune to do jobs for great thought leaders; I mean the big names. I needed the big boys in my client base. But it didn't happen that way. I prayed, prayer never made it happen. So don't confuse spirituality for stupidity. I went to work. I kept designing, writing, and showcasing my work. Gradually, I can say my work began to grow into a global standard, one that can compete in the market anywhere. People began to send work to me to compare with what they were offered by others, I began to receive testimonials and reviews for my work. That was when the kind of calls I have always dreamed of started coming in, requesting for my services. Some would just want me to develop concepts and idea for their book and allow them do the rest. My friend, It's a journey and growth must take place. This year I had the opportunity of working with two international authors. This is a big win for me.

In the church ministry I see a lot of young people like me, getting frustrated when they are not getting access to preach for larger crowds or "big pulpits." They get worried because the "fat envelops" haven't started coming in (by the way, you don't preach for the money). They don't know that even Jesus grew in all ramification before he could step out and speak in so many places. Why did He wait for 30 years? What was He doing? Failure to comprehend this truth has made a lot of desperate folks seek for alternative source of power to enhance miracle, enlarge membership and finances. You don't need to be told; the end is shameful.

Growth is a life principle that many don't understand. Growth on its own brings opportunities. Why did I say so? There are clients you can't get when you start your business. It will take you years or months of consistent work, to be able to deliver the kind of service and product that they would like to pay for. This is why I said one good job done will lead you to another opportunity. It's like a chain. There are platforms that will not receive you until your work has grown into the type that can stand there. You cant just start talking today and tomorrow, you want to become a TEDex speaker.

If you are looking for an opportunity to maximize your potential, then growth is your answer. The leadership expert John C Maxwell, in his book *How successful people grow* said, "if you focus on goals, you may hit the goals-but that doesn't guarantee growth. But if you focus on growth, you will always hit the goals."[7]

KEY AREAS OF GROWTH TO MAGNET OPORTUTNITIES.

There are key areas of your life that must grow if you want to be the kind of person that magnets opportunities daily, especially in this part of the globe. They are many, but I will be dealing with 5 of them. Each of them will greatly determine the results you get. What are they?

1. Mindset: Broaden your perspective.

You can't think, like a local champion and expect to attract a global opportunity. The world doesn't revolve around your village. You attract things on the level of your thoughts. You can't do business with certain people if you still think like that vast majority of the world's population. What do I mean by this? Let me explain. For example, I am from the eastern part of Nigeria and like every other ethnic group, we've had our own wars, differences and lots more.

But if you hold onto that and use it as a criteria to decide who you talk to, walk with, do business with, or listen to, you will greatly miss a lot.

Most of us grew up with hatred for other ethnic groups; hatred passed to us by our parents and environment or community. And it has affected how we relate with others, how we do business with them and whether or not we have serious commitment with them.

I was on a bus one day and two people were having a heated argument about the state of the nation, the political opinion and loyalty of a particular ethic group and one of the men said, *i will never do business or trust a Yoruba man*. I smiled and immediately asked, "what if a person from that tribe is your door to the opportunity that will change your life forever?" And everywhere was silent. That was when I began to give my own lecture and share my thoughts about having a broad perspective in life.

Just like Bishop Thomas Dexter Jakes once said, "the ravens doesn't go to church but they fed Elijah." The key to the door you have been trying to open might not be from your ethnic group, he or she might not look like one from your religious sect. It's very possible that they might not believe in the same thing you believe in, but **God has a way of using people to answer other peoples prayers whether they are religious or not**. That is how life opportunities work also. The opportunities you seek will never say "oh, kingsley is a Nigerian, so I must use a Nigerian to introduce myself to him." Your opportunity- ladder can come from anywhere, any place, any tribe, any religious sect, you can think of. You need to let go of the hate and biased mindset, and broaden your perspective to attract opportunities to yourself.

Your parent's differences with a certain tribe or particular religious sect is not yours to inherit; it is not wealth.

Broaden your perspective.

One day I was with my pastor; Pastor Biodun Ajibade. While we were discussing after an outreach, he shared a story that made me believe that opportunity doesn't know religion, denomination, tribe or nationality. According to him, a pastor whom he knew personally completed his church building, but could not roof it because of the size of the church; the church couldn't afford the money to roof the just completed building.

One day, a man walked into the church and requested to see the pastor. He came out and the "stranger" said "while I was working there, God told me to come and roof this church."

"We don't have the money", the pastor replied. "No, I didn't mean you should pay me, I will roof it all by myself." True to his words, the man roofed the church without a dime from them. The mystery man was from another religion.

Opportunities doesn't not come in the raiment you recognize. It won't come from your favorite persons or people. It can choose to come in any form. Hating people will rob you of the good they can bring into your life. Broaden your mind. Think love. Think global.

Stop inheriting hatred against a tribe from your parents, it is not wealth or riches.

Your mindset determine the doors you have access to. This affects a lot of religious and "spiritual" people in Africa too. A lot of us believe that anyone who is not born again is their enemy and they should only do business, or listen to people in church. And this I believe is because we don't really understand what *church means.* My friend, **when church is identified primarily with a building, it soon turns centripetal in its focus and everything on the outside becomes adversarial, turning the city and the market place into enemies that have to be subdued, destroyed or avoided. This leads to a state of animosity, if not all-out war, against the cities we live in and its central components; business, education and government.** This attitude denies many of the opportunities that lay waste in the nation.

You will continue to walk in narrow paths where things, resources, breakthrough are limited if you continue to think in a narrow way. The world doesn't revolve around your ethnic group, your denomination, your village, and certainly not even what your father told you when you were growing up. Even fathers can be wrong. Gray hair doesn't always mean wisdom. Information can be outdated. You need to broaden your perspective. **Develop the kind of mindset that is not threatened by differences; one that accommodates peoples differences.**

Another area you need to grow if you must become a person that magnets opportunities is;

2. Relational ability/Relationship Capacity.

One of the strongest triggers of opportunities are people. So relating with people is of utmost importance.

Becoming the type of person that attracts opportunities at ease is not about doing your very best. It is also about your relationship with others; how you could work together with them, how your gifts and abilities complete and complement others. One of the most important thing you can do to become an opportunity magnet is develop the ability to build long term relationship with people. It was Zig Ziglar that said "if you will help others get what they want, they will help you get everything you need in life. To attract opportunities, you must intentionally cultivate your relationships, add value to others.

No man was born with a perfect inherent ability to handle their fellow human. We all grow in the way we relate with people. Time and experience helps us get better. **Understanding that the opportunity you are seeking will come from a man like you, makes you conscious of your dealing with men.**

You will need to learn how to relate with people better if you want to get the best from people. You need to master inter personal relation. Learn to deal with people in wisdom, not based on how they make you feel (may be angry), what you heard about them, what you think of them based on what they wear, drive, eat, where they come from or where they live. Be wise. If your relationship with people is parasitic, they will hardly open certain doors to you. Love and giving is a two way thing.

The year 2019 has been a great year of learning for me. Recently, I succeeded in completely uninstalling a particular mindset that was programmed within me as a child which I never knew also had a serious effect as to the opportunities that come my way. In Nigeria for example, as children most of us were told not to talk to strangers. Our parents made it look like every stranger you meet is bad, capable of using you for "blood money," can turn you into and abstract object and possibly use you as a sacrifice to whatever god they worship. Most of us were even told to never greet people we don't know or respond to them when they talk to us.

Dr. Ubong King, in one of his teaching on Business growth and wealth creation taught about the law of penetration in business and one of the key things emphasized is *the law of penetrating strangers.* Your next business deal is in the hands of someone. Your next appointment or contract is in the hands of a person. It is not in heaven (This is not declaring independence from God). God doesn't keep contracts in heaven neither does he save business deals there. You might not even know this person. They might not be from your church, or faith. They might not even look like what you like, but truth is, your money is in the hands of people. I really believe if some church folks understand this, they will stop harassing God with the "bless me or I die" kind of prayer.

Learn to connect with people. I have since then, used this strategy and it has really helped me as an author. I have succeeded in many times selling and giving out my books to people whom I never knew before. And it kick started a great relationship and brought speaking opportunities. Above all, it has afforded me the opportunities to positively affect the lives of many people whom I never taught I could reach from my small corner.

Opportunities are everywhere and comes every day. Only few people have the sight to recognize it. Social media and the internet has been very helpful to the growth of my business as a publisher and a freelance writer in 2018 to 2019. Just an ordinary *hello* and *Hi,* have sparked up great conversation with strangers and has led us to strike publishing deals and build great relationship even when we have not seen each other. Your next opportunities is with another person, and if you don't learn how to connect with people, you will not have access to it. What might be holding your opportunity could be your inability to build great relationships.

Gatekeepers are real.

While talking to a friend on the phone one day, he narrated to me how someone gave him a life time opportunity just because of his previous dealing with another person. He ended our conversation with one statement, "Kingsley, be careful how you treat or relate with people, **gate keepers are real." There are things you can't change with prayer and a bad name is one of them.** There are no actions that go unnoticed or unrecorded in this life. If you live carelessly, it's only a matter of time, you will be trapped by the results of your careless or unguarded actions towards other people. There were times in my life when I never knew about these things I am sharing with you now.

You don't have the right to treat any man badly. Actions are recorded and there are gate keepers standing at the door of your next opportunity. **One bad report can destroy your chances of getting or accessing an opportunity you have been dreaming, praying and hoping for**. A perfect example is seen in the story I shared earlier about Nnamdi. If you can learn to treat every person you come across as your ladder to the next level, you will minimize your chances of losing opportunities.

If you must let go of a relationship, do it appropriately. If you must "fire your boss," fire him according to the books. Don't be deceived, his name or recommendation might be the key that opens your next door.

Be wise!

3. Problem solving ability

The school system teaches us how life and opportunities work.

Have you noticed that the door of a higher class is only opened for you when you pass the examinations and test of the present class? Think about that for a minute. This tells you that as you solve the present level challenge, you become qualified for the next level. You see this even in games. As you conquer one level, you move to the next and the rewards also increases.

Doors open to people who solve problems. To access more open doors/opportunities, one of the key things you need to develop is your problem solving ability. Have you noticed that in the corporate or business world, people are not promoted for how long they have worked in an organization? They are not promoted because the HR manager and the board of directors like their faces. People who have a tract record of solving problems, valuable people are the ones promoted. Doors of bigger offices only open to people who has grown and shows capacity to handle bigger task. Growth is the game changer my friend. **If all you do to get promoted in the office is fasting, you will never have it. Even God doesn't reward unfaithfulness, irresponsibility and unproductivity**. Anyone faithful in little, receives more. There is a protocol. Serve, deliver value in the organization and you set yourself up for promotion; you put yourself on the frontline for career breakthrough.

If you want to access more opportunities, you need to be good at problem solving. Everything is not solved using prayer and fasting. I don't want to sound anti-religious, anti-Christian or anti- prayer, but it's the truth. **You will need to learn how to use your brain**. God didn't decorate your brain with tissues for nothing. It is for a purpose.

4. Speaking ability/ Conversational ability

Learning how to speak, starting and keeping great conversations is one way you open yourself up for opportunities. I said earlier that opportunities are everywhere around us. But it only takes a person with great sight to recognize them. And learning how to speak and keep conversation is one good way to make it happen anywhere.

Some people have sealed business deals with people they are meeting for the first time on a flight. How did this happen? Learn how to talk. Some persons have gotten new clients on the train by just learning how to converse.

There are skills you need to have. Ability to communicate effectively is one of them. Learning how to create good inter personal relationship is one of them.

What would you do if I tell you that the stranger sitting next to you can be the door way to your mega breakthrough? You can't tell God how to bless you. You can't tell him where to keep the blessing you have been praying for. He might keep it in Zarephat, and if you stay in Jericho, you will wait all your life. **Some persons we come across daily are strategically positioned for our lifting;** whether spiritual, business, financial or mental. You just need to learn how to connect and talk.

There are so many doors that can open up for you if you learn how to speak, whether on a platform, to individuals, or to the man sitting next to you.

5. Marketing ability.

I have always thought that marketing is selling goods and services only. But I have come to understand that it is beyond that. It is about sharing an idea, promoting a solution, and promoting a school of thought. It's not just about goods and services but yourself too. If you don't learn or grow your marketing skill, there are certain doors that will not open for you. For certain employment opportunities to open for you as a young graduate, you need to learn how to market yourself.

How can you be positioned before an organization and make yourself so invaluable that they will not want to miss having you on their team? This is also marketing. Often, those who are recognized are really not people with the best of skills, best of style, best of everything but those who were able to market themselves appropriately.

Everyone is a marketer. You must learn how to sell yourself to people, organization and create the right perception that would make them yearn to have you work with them, or do business with them.

SKILL UP

We cannot talk about attracting opportunities in this era without a mention of skills. I have always believed that school is not a system to distribute, collect or store information by a given course of knowledge. It is a system to inform, inspire and reform a man to become resourceful, creative and productive. And this results finds expression through the skills you build whether in or out of the four walls of a school.

Go beyond being talented. Talent is not enough, skill is a plus. Acquire skills in your area of pursuit. There are opportunities that you can't enjoy except you have the skill to match the requirements.

You need skills and in this internet age, almost all skills are learnable just by a click.

Growth is a key factor in attracting opportunities.

I would like to take us to the next level which I believe is closely related to this last point I just made. See you on the other page.

CHAPTER SEVEN

SHOW YOUR WORK

Gold is not appreciated in the dark.

No man, when he hath lighted a candle, putteth it in a secret place, neither under a bushel, but on a candlestick, that they which come in may see the light. [7]

Do you know you can make opportunity discover you?

Earlier I said that opportunity has behavior. Now I am saying that opportunity has eyes; she can see. She can see those who are ready, and those who are not.

She can see those who are hungry to get her and those who are busy just wishing.

Engage your hands.

How can you make opportunity discover you?

You must have a work you are doing. The best way to magnet opportunity is not sitting idle and wishing for it to come, but working with what your hands find at the moment while you daily expect the big one to show up. Many of us young people complain of not having a job, the government not providing employment and so many other things. Truth is, we have passed that time in our nation where our hopes are left hanging on the shoulders of those in political positions. Your life was never designed to be run by the government. You must find something doing. No matter how little it is, do something. Don't say there is no job out there, even if it means selling by the road side, do it. Even if it means driving taxi, do it with your vision and hope intact. It is more honorable than sitting idle and even better than stealing or begging.

Stop sitting idle in the name of waiting on God. That is not really faith. this is where most folks get it wrong.

Own whatever it is you're doing.

Don't be ashamed of what you do. There is dignity in labour. Internet fraud is not the best way to build lasting riches or wealth. It is not an honourable way of living. Do good works no matter how little it is. It is unfortunate that our society today make certain means of honourable living look small and demeaning.

For there is no man that doeth anything in secret, and he himself seeketh to be known openly. If thou do these things, shew thyself to the world.[8]

Show yourself.

When we were much younger, when a teacher asks a question in class and we are consistently answering those questions, our peers begin to see us as people who think they know all. They tag us all sorts of names. Some call you "sabi sabi", some say "I too know-ITK." For many people, these names get to them and whenever a question is asked, even though they have the answers, they keep quiet for fear of being ridiculed by their class mates. Do you know some of us grow into adulthood with the same mental programming and it becomes difficult for us to share our expertise, products, experiences and stories because we fear been ridiculed, or seen as proud and pompous. Well, there is a big line between arrogance and confidence. This mental programing makes some of us adults get scared of showing off what we can do for fear of what people will say. This is what I call self-hindering factor.

Austin Kleon in his book *Steal Like an Artist* said, that, "the not-so-secret formula for getting known and attracting opportunities is simple- do good works and share it."[9] Show case what you can do to the world. If David only played his strings in a hidden place as many assume, how did someone know he was a skillful player and recommended him to King Saul when there was a need for a skillful player at the Kings palace (I Samuel 16:16-18). Think about that my friend.

If you are a good singer or a song writer waiting for an opportunity to come, let me show you something better than waiting. It is simple. Do good work and share it. Show your work. Before now, it will take years for opportunity to see you, but now,

she can see you by just a click. You have produced **a good love song** and you don't have money for promotion. Option one, here is one way you can make the promotion come to you. Simply, look out for weddings, arrange a meeting with the couples, tell them you have a song and you would love to come and play for them on their wedding. Tell them you are doing this free of charge. Many might turn you down, but for the few who would say yes to your offer, make sure you over perform. I repeat, over perform. Make sure you go there with your CD or business card and good camera for coverage. Post the videos and photos to your social media platforms with great caption. (#wedding performance) As you play from one wedding to another, you are pushing your song into people's ears. Many others will want to have you come play for their wedding or their friends weddings too. Over time, you can begin to put a fee to your appearance at a wedding. Try this and thank me later.

Option two. Use your social media platforms to perform live for people. Here, people will watch you do your thing from the comfort of their homes. This means you are no longer waiting for them to see you. You are putting yourself in their face to see you. make them see you.

Geography is no longer your enemy.

Thanks to the internet, because of it, geography is no longer our enemy. Put your work out there for the world to see. It is not pride. Some religious teaching has made us belittle ourselves, our gifts and creative ability and worse still keep us stagnant leaving us with the impression that it's the work of the enemy. Put your work out there on the internet and watch people see the amazing things you can do from the comfort of their bedroom. The social media is one of the most powerful platforms available now, and as a young person you need to maximize it if you want opportunities to run to you.

Position yourself to be discovered. In this age, everyone has a microphone. What you do with yours determines the result you get.

You are a writer, bless the souls of people with the transformational piece you write. Share your own unique story and journey. This is why Facebook and other social media platforms is now the new place for auditions. (If you know what I mean) Don't keep shouting "I am a writer" in your bedroom, yet no one sees what you write. Step out and let us see you. You have been praying "father let my helpers locate me," now I am showing you how to locate your helpers.

If you are in business, share your process, share your finished work, and share the feedbacks and testimonials clients have given. Let people know you are good at what you do. There are many people around you who don't know what you do, and yet they need same service. Guess what! They take the money they are supposed to pay you and give to another person. Show your work, and let opportunity see you. When she does, she will come to you.

What if my work is not good enough you say. We don't put our works out there because they're perfect. It's also a means of growing. In the words of Austin Kleon, "The Internet can be more than just a resting place to publish your finished ideas- -it can also be an incubator for ideas that aren't fully formed, a birthing center for developing work that you haven't started yet," and let me add, " a learning center where you learn better ways to do things." May be you are worried about people stealing your ideas. The more open you are about sharing your passions, the closer people will feel to your work. There's no penalty for revealing your secrets. People love it when you give your secrets away, and sometimes, if you're smart about it, they'll reward you by buying the things you're selling. By the way, you can control what you share. But make sure you share something if you want to be seen. It is not pride to say to the world, "hey I can do this." David said to the Israelites "Hey, I can kill this giant." That's not pride. Don't let anyone tell you;

"You too dey show yourself."

By the way, if you don't show yourself, how would the world know you exist? There are certain opportunities that will not come to you. Humility and low self-esteem don't look alike. Be bold to share your work.

It is disheartening to see young people who are living in the best time ever, waste away their time and lives, yet blaming it on the government, society, families and their churches/religion. The best time to live is now. Imagine having a free university like YouTube. Imagine being able to learn anything, I mean anything from your bedroom. You can practically learn everything you need there. I mean almost everything. All you need to pay is your time and data. But what we get is almost nothing. Young people spend time that could be invested into skill acquisition and application to solve real life problems, in having all manner of dirty conversation online, posting nudes, going into vocal war with each other regarding political views and lamenting over bad government. Some spend their data month after month watching jokes and porn sites, as if to say porn pays their bills.

As a young African, position yourself to be seen by the world. Opportunity doesn't live in your village alone. It can come from anywhere. And one place you can find her any time in this dispensation is on the internet. Do not be afraid to share your works. Do good works and show it to the world. No one lights a candle and puts it under the table. That's exactly what Jesus said. You and I were created for good works and I believe it doesn't just stop at soul winning.

Talented people are not discovered in their bedroom. Why do you think people organize talent hunts and shows? It is for the purpose of making a star discovered. You are a star. There are many people who would not have the opportunity of becoming who they are today if they didn't show what they were capable of doing; they unveiled their gifting to the world and the world is calling on them now.

Share your story.

Each of us has a great, unfinished story. Your own narratives weaves together the story of past life-shaping events, vital current experiences, and inspiring dreams about the future. This will bring certain opportunities your way and set you on global platforms. Don't wait till the story is perfect. Your life is a blog and not a book; update daily.

It is not about having a really great story or the usual rags to riches kind of story. It's not even about the whole story. It's about *your* story-your pivotal life events that impact your present but does not limit your future. These are key things that open doors for you with ease.

In addition to showing your work, you need to embrace consistency. You need to be consistent. Result will not come from doing something just once. Just like losing weight. You don't lose weight by going to the gym once or following a particular diet for one day. It is through consistency that the end result is manifested.

Remember that opportunity will not come to you with a siren. You don't have to live in America to get opportunities and open doors in America. It can happen even while you are living in Nigeria. All you need to do is show your work. Come out and let the world see you.

CHAPTER EIGHT

SERVICE

It is not easy for a man who has not served to be served. To receive you must give, and to get support, you must give support. - Elisha Mamman

There are many persons who believe that Africa or Nigeria in this case doesn't have the enabling environment or system to hatch the ideas of young people. Because of this, they assume that success in the African society is nearly impossible. I don't quite agree. Well, even if you think the environment isn't designed in such a way that it gives platform for young ones, there are ways that are proven which when followed, can take one up the success ladder.

Service is one of such ways.

In the words of Elisha Mamman, "it is better to serve something worthwhile than to hold on to something worthless. It is better to serve something moving, than to hold on to something that died the very day it started."

If you want to enjoy exceptional opportunities, one best way to do so is to volunteer to help pursue a good cause. I mean service. Service is a high way to the top. You have to come to a point where you start looking beyond just yourself and your personal vision and pursuits. We are all children of one father, fighting one enemy trying to devour humanity. Serve your community, serve your organization, serve in the church, and serve people. Serve with your time, energy, resources and in any capacity you can.

The reason many are walking the streets, yet seem not to be finding opportunities is because they have lost **the art of service**. We have so many socially dead young people and that is why they cannot tap into opportunities. In the words of Samson Adah Paul, **"biological death is for a man to disengage from breath. Spiritual death is for a man to disengage**

from God and social death is for a man to disengage from service."[10]

A man disconnects himself from opportunities when he disconnects himself from service. Yielding yourself to service is simply becoming a human seed. By this I mean, a commitment to rob yourself of your rights and privileges, in order to bear the responsibility of cultivating your energy, ideas to bear the fruit of solutions for the benefit of mankind. To be a human seed is to willingly, sacrificially and ceaselessly deprive yourself of social comfort, convenience, pleasure and indulgence in other to employ your potential to enhance human existence.

In his book *Atomic Knowledge*, Samson Adah Paul explained that there are certain opportunities that will never come to you no matter how you pray and fast for it until you have made yourself a human seed. **The great destiny God has planned out for you is beyond what you can eat, drink and wear.** It is operating from a global standpoint. And the only time you can magnet the opportunity to step into such is when you plant yourself as a seed in a particular field of service.

Go in and fully devote yourself to a good cause. Pursue after national transformation. The moment you put yourself out there to help others in their pursuits to change the nation or move an organization forward, you are simply positioning yourself to be helped too. This is one way to kill selfishness which I believe has ravished us in Africa. Learn to live beyond "what is in it for me." There is more you can get if you position yourself to give and serve.

God never designed us to be containers. We are channels. Make your hands, body, mouth, and even resources, a channel through which help will reach other people for the greater good of mankind. By so doing, you are attracting help to yourself.

If you look at the African society today, look at Nigeria today, look at the church, the art of genuine service to the cause of God, the good cause of men, is almost lost. Yes we still have few willing and yielded but it's not enough when compared to the millions out there who are supposed to be doing it.

Learn to serve. Become a *SERVE-ANT*.

FINAL THOUGHTS

It's time to arise and make things happen in your life. This is a clarion call to every Young Nigerian out there. We need to wake up.

You have been given unlimited power.

Wielding that power for result is a choice you have to make. Opportunity is a function of awareness.

No matter your present state, my friend you can rise from the ashes. Everything I have shared in this book are practical guides, not some theoretical concepts. Some I have used too many times and they are bringing results and I'm still practicing and getting better in them too. If you can practice three out of everything said already, you will have amazing results.

There is no special day designed for opportunities to locate people. It can be today. It can be NOW. Remember that success does not have a time keeper.

Opportunities doesn't come once in a life time. Every day you wake up, you have a million and one opportunities to do and become what you have never imagined. You need to see it with your mind's eye for you to hold it. It's a mindset. When you tell yourself that opportunity only comes once in a lifetime, you shut your mind from recognizing one when it shows up.

Everything you do can be a door-way to that great opportunity you have been praying and looking for. Treat every business with utmost seriousness. There is no small business, neither is there small job. There is nothing like a small client. No matter how much you are paid, deliver excellently. One job well done can bring you before the right person.

Money should not be the only reward you get for doing a job. Don't live for the cash you get. Personally, I strive not to get **just cash** after every job done, I go for cash and recommendation. I believe that cash alone is the lowest form of reward. Every job should lead you to another better and bigger opportunity.

Treat everyone you come across in life good. No matter how poorly dressed they are, they can be your ladder to the next level. Everyone won't treat you right. I totally understand that. We can't completely eradicate stupidity form everyone one in the world.

The widow of zarephat was just a widow, yet through her the prophet Elijah was preserved. The raven is one of the stingiest creatures who doesn't even care for its own young ones, yet was the vessel God used to feed the prophet Elijah. The people God has destined to be your ladder to great platforms might not look like it. They might not have your theology, but they are certainly your ladder.

Every opportunity you have to teach, deliver or speak, do it excellently. There is no small speaking engagement. There is no small platform. Your lifting might be seated in that place you call small auditorium. Don't look down on people, they are your door to the next platform.

Stop running from problems and start solving them when you see one (and note that you can't solve every problem). The world open doors for problem solvers. The world recognizes problem solvers. We were designed by God to solve problems; individual, family, societal, religious etc. You are not disadvantaged.

There are doors that can only be opened to you when you grow. This means the dividing line between you and some opportunities is simply growth.

And don't forget that gold is not appreciated in the dark. It must be seen in the light.

Come out and shine your light.

I see us changing the world together.

ABOUT THE AUTHOR

Kingsley Obiefule, an author and a speaker, is a human development strategist, endowed with local context actionable content; on a mission to help young people break self-limiting beliefs, and Spiral up with peak productivity as their end result. He strongly believes that one can be turned into a multitude if given the right tool of training and if knowledge is engaged through creative thinking and actions.

He is the Chief-Editor and mission director of the **INSPIRE AFRICA MAGAZINE**, a Campus Revolution publication designed for African Universities and High School students; with the mission to inspire growth & Transformation within the lives of young students and equip them with the right tool to stand out in their various spheres, changing others and collaboratively building the nation.

With over 7 result proven books, he is a consultant and a publisher; the Creative Director of HOPEALIFE Publishing. He is also the author of *Village People & Goliath Move your Shit.*

He resides in Kaduna, Nigeria.

You can reach me via 07060969059. You can also connect with me via any social media platform.

END NOTES

1. Isolate and Destroy- Korede Komaiya 2013 Published by Ezra Media
2. Psalm_68:19
3. Jacobs Porridge- Temple Nwoke
4. Where there is problem, there is money- Sunday Adelajah 2017, Evangel Publishers, Kaduna.
5. Life's challenges your opportunities- John Hagee, Charisma House 2009
6. Atomic Knowledge- Adah Paul, Identity Books 2015
7. How successful people grow-John C Maxwell, Hachette books 2014.
8. Luke 11:33
9. **John 7:4** King James Version of the Bible

10.	Steal like an Artist Austin Kleon- WorkMan Publishing Company, New York.

11.	Atomic Knowledge-Creativity at the speed of shock- Samson Adah Paul, Identity Books 2015.

APPRECIATION

No one becomes all they are supposed to be without the contribution of other people in their life. To be where I am now, I have enjoyed wonderful contribution from great people whether far or near. And for this I am really grateful. They are too many to mention.

To my wonderful pastors, Biodun Ajibade and Danjuma Amos, your teachings help me become better.

Dr. Ubong King, your social media pages and books are chronicles of wisdom that is capable of rewiring and repositioning any man for greatness. Thank you for all you do Sir.

To my wonderful Team at HOPEALIFE PUBLISHING, indeed, you have been a great help and support system. Thank You.

And to you reading now, I love you from my heart.